THAW

Charles Bennett

Fair Acre Press

First published in Great Britain in September, 2018 by Fair Acre Press
www.fairacrepress.co.uk

A CIP catalogue record for this book is available from the British
Library

ISBN 978-1-911048-33-6

Printed and bound by Lightning Source
Lightning Source has received Chain of Custody (CoC) certification
from:
The Forest Stewardship CouncilTM (FSC®)
Programme for the Endorsement of Forest CertificationTM (PEFCTM)
The Sustainable Forestry Initiative® (SFI®).

Typeset by Nadia Kingsley
Cover Design by Algimantas Murza

Cover image © CarryAckroyd 2018

The epigraph for 'Foxglove' is taken from:
A Modern Herbal Mrs. M. Grieve. Dover 1971

for Phillippa, Carly-Anne and Bella

CONTENTS

Death of a Wasp

Zero moments drown me. I forget
how to play the garden's green music.

I dozed under gutters or lapped the cool
windowsill's luscious wood. Let me show you

wind-fallen pears, hollowed into stumps
of succulence. Sweetness completes me now

by three carious bricks and an overgrown fence.
This nothing I must swallow down until I am full

tastes of snow. It is time to be still and silent;
time to become a shadow.

My poison is a drop of gold in the slow light.
Beneath my feet the leaf is letting go.

Planting Apricots

This spring perhaps,
I'll stretch a stave of wires along
that southern-facing wall,

(Victorian bricks, blanched
to acid ochres and flame-gold oxides,
friable and kiln-split

with the craquelure of firing)
then plant, for the sake of sweetness
on my tongue in early autumn,

a row of apricots along it:
New Large Early or maybe Alfred –
I'd hear you laugh at the end

of a long hot day, as I call:
I'm just going out to water Alfred!
Left over right and under,

I'll fasten the pliant stems
with kiss-knots of twine, training
their fingers out to form

an espalier or fan, like a child's
drawing of the sun: radices of growth,
obedient fronds that drowse

against a length of scorched wall.
When I look at the trees I'll be reading
a florid language – swollen nodes

of flower-buds punctuate the stem,
as if each bleb were a word on the line
of the branch. Does a tree speak

in fresh consonant leaves
and flowered vowels; should we
have been listening more

and listening harder? Perhaps
it would help if we were plants like them,
if we danced with xylem and phloem

from breathing light, if now
and then we burst into quiet splendour.
Unable to blossom ourselves,

we invented the garden.
Aiming to quell and countermand the dread
that dogs our days and may come true,

we plant a bright music
that's yet to come but is almost here;
a charge of ripeness held and kept

in a sprig of speckled fruit –
as though we might taste in their succulence
(fuzzed and tinged with a breath

of burnt-sienna and terracotta)
green leaves opening into radiance –
the arrival of soft time.

The Poet's Childhood

When I was two night's old I fell into a book.
I sank past squonking geese and a chuntering tractor,
seven black cows and a tame crow,
eleven sheep the colour of deep midnight
and a cockerel who wheezed a lullaby.

When I came to the bottom of the book
and bumped my head, I knew what to do:
I began to swallow its pages one by one –
first a squall of jackdaws, then a witch's cat,
and a sow like a lake of treacle.

I saved myself from drowning by drinking the pond.
I gulped the house with its one lighted window,
the churns, the pails, the troughs, the dog's bowl.
A farmyard nevertheless thereafter my wherewithal –
its creatures crying out in dark voices.

The Street

I'd have the street less straight –
      if only to let each canted gable
downspout, doorstep, windowsill,
      resonate
in crooked tones by turns until
      an unintended madrigal
is wound within a bend.
      As woodnotes in the blackbird's song
discover a tranquil way to end
      (where improvised mellifluence
can take its place – at one among
      the various)
so may accidental turnings
      lead me to the happenstance
which lets me find this corner is
      a corner at the heart of things,
where all my errors right me as
      (peculiar and curious)
the weight and place
      of each missed step
combine to trip
      me into grace.

Questions for an Amoeba

Sloppy translucent egg in a glass frying pan,
        puddle with a heart like a pebble –

whatever arrives you allow it to fall through
        and do not mind what it is,

because as you let it go, it makes you what you are.
        When I drew you in a diagram at school

were you trying to show me I must learn
        to pull my heart in half

and sail on the given breeze of my own breath?
        Deliquescent seed that needs no root

you blossom and pulse and gather on your own release
        like the swirl of starlings overhead

when I did my homework. If I master the ways to melt
        in a dance of collapse, if I pour myself away

to become a lake, will I know at last if you
        are the eye of water or the tear it cries?

Questions for Snakelocks Anemone

Your long green fronds are tipped with pink
      like a nest of slim leaves or soft roots.

You clutch the bright thoughts that come and go
      in the clear mind of water.

On the midnight of low tide you curl and flex
      (dreaming perhaps a dance of deft convulsions)

until this passing cloud and distant sail
      are fed into the landscape of your soul.

If I let my hair grow long and swallow the tide
      will I learn to distinguish at last

between what I need to let go, or hold onto?
      Will the moon be salty on my tongue;

and might I come to comprehend the sea
      by staying still and letting it all wash over?

At night the stars would be moments that went to my making –
      I'd stretch my arms to gather in their light.

Bivalve Seashells of the Northern European Seas

When you nuzzle the pad of your thumb
    in the glint where I lay, can you tell

how I listened to the sea, and swallowed the notes
    of pollen night by night, until I became a song?

I am there in the cleft of your brain and the salt of a tear,
    in the heart shaking hands with itself.

I am two going in to one with nothing left over.
    I flex down the middle like a book on a hinge of breath.

Showing you how to blossom with two petals
    I glisten like the iridescent wings of a sea-butterfly.

Man Rescued from Sinking Iceberg

Out of the frost-heave waves,
out of the freeze-marrow sea brimful
with flotsam in bobbing archipelagos,

they pluck me sodden with shivers
into the cork-floated self-righting lifeboat
for a Drink This tot and a blanket.

As they hoist me aboard to a cheer
the ship is a Dover cliff in summer moonlight.
After the captain's handshake and sweet tea

I watch her white hull slip into oblivion.
You nearly caught your death I hear them say,
and then in these soft sheets I slowly drown.

The Blackbird at Aberbach

From a garden at the end of Wales
my radio lands a glimmering song in Irish –

plangent and lithe it trembles
like an angel overheard by the aerial.

And all at once I am Caliban
floated on a slow wave of melodic swell,

wondering how this cadence
has flown across the water on soft wings.

And so when a blackbird arrives
in a fluster of dark feathers on a nearby rowan

and starts a duet with the radio
as if he were tuning in to a station for birds –

I wonder if he hasn't come over
from the garden of a cottage in Glanmore

where Prospero is humming to himself
as a spell of yellow music opens the evening.

Seagulls

I saw a drift of seagulls swerve
        on a thermal

a loose white spiral
        they sauntered round an indolent

circumfluence
        as if they rode and rested on a weave

of air. Stable
        and yet provisional

gathered by its own escape
        the waft

of their unravelment
        was a gift

of white wings in a blue sky –
        and I sensed the warm thrum of a self-spun gyroscope

as it kept me steady
        with turbulence.

The Leaf

For a moment, I think it's a butterfly –
      this leaf twirled up on the waft of an autumn gale.

I watch it lift and spin past my office window
      till it trembles overhead like a skylark.

As twenty-thousand reasons to put the clocks back
      ride on a big *scoosh* of chilly wind, I wonder

perhaps if I gathered those brittle creatures,
      and hung them back on their branches one by one

(like counting summer's broken numbers
      down to a green zero and starting again)

would it all come right in the end –
      or is perhaps this vision of leaves falling upwards

a sign to say the pieces of all those days
      are flown each night on a glimmer of yellow wings?

The Storm

I left these bedclothes on the line last night
       in a summer thunderstorm –
              they took all day to dry.

And now, as I am lost among the sheets
       the quilt and pillowslips, I sense
              the bulk and drench of dark

that ruined these blues to purple,
       trickle and lick along my spine –
              until the capillaries of my skull

hold their fill: and I am charged and saturate
       with all the inclement rush and pull
              of difficult weather I have known.

Yet count it my good luck to lie
       where glittering stems of twisted light
              fleck me with their clarity –

like cadences which ululate their murmur
       on the inner ear, I'm freshened
              by a thunder-bruise that blossoms

into ease: a quietude which lingers and clings
       like drops of light on a holly leaf;
              or in the night-sky of the head

glimmers irreducibly – an unexpected aftermath
       distilled from a frown of clouds, filling
              this empty rain-butt to the brim.

Borrowed Light

One spent petal on the kitchen table
where six buttermilk roses bend their necks
      like swans on a oval lake.

The bedroom ceiling charged
with first snow – as you wonder:
      Why have we woken up so early?

Spilt on blurred gardens after dusk
from windows with their curtains left undrawn
      it's cream with a tinge of blue.

The puddle's icy meniscus.
A wood stippled with yellow at level sun.
      The car with its stubble of lichen.

Like a congress of wrens in their clench
of pressed heads, it's a hive of candles
      brightened against winter,

a blackbird's shadow danced
across the grass, the icicle's song
      grown from cold notes.

The frowning moon as she pales
and brightens from neap to perihelion.
      A waterbutt solid with summer.

It's an underside of wings above the town
as a flock skids and skates on the overcast.
      Petal-clouds who blush with going... going...

It's the stiff of frosted cotton
left on the line, a face on the pillow
          with the sheen of wood anemones.

Headlights along the hillside.
The scent of sloes pricked with a silver pin.
          A snowdrop budding in your throat.

The River Wedding

He was her frog and she his April shower
their kisses a delicious sparge of summer rain.

Her bouquet was a lake of water-lilies –
all honeymoon they were drenched.

                    *

After the flood their wedding photos
fetch up in riverside hedges smiling like billy-oh.

In moonlight the quiet stream
is a white dress drifting underwater.

Shovelling the Snow

He snouts the pig-snort blade
in a push of grunting. It clears its throat
to wake me with a iron growl.

Like the clank of a winter clock,
it coughs a fit of scrapes. He shoves the sharp dog
to bark a deep path from our front door.

I look down now to wonder what he's planting
and see him scuff a neat, white topsoil of heavy cloud
to open a dark absence I'll follow him down.

In a track of measured melting, glistened with salt,
he has made his own spring along our drive.
He waves and goes next door

to rasp the flags at old Mr Ridgeway's house.
Afterwards hung in the shed on its own nail
it drips the cold gleam of being struck.

Thaw

Icicles weep – drainpipes puther:
  this time of year there's a sniff in the weather.

Our shiver's gone flat, the sky is a haze,
  the calendar's numbers have been erased.

We pull off Before and shrug into After
  when pavements shall, at last, be softer.

Here is a shift of tense to show
  snowdrops under the mistletoe.

Hung-over, we surface with no plans –
  remove our gloves: hold hands.

We warm the key with a dancing flame
  open the day and start for home;

flex our brollies, dust off a song –
  listen for the first lawnmower of spring.

The Moon Toad

What does it taste of I wonder –
the sinew of this curse you chew as if
            you can never be full. Pale as the bones of stars
            you lodge on my winter doorstep.

This is the buckled torso of an old snowman:
his job is to sharpen rain. Fat with cold
            he squats as grit-spattered wind
            kicks the puckered sack of his grimy skin.

If you spoke a bitter word, would your croak
be the quick snap of brittle bones that never mend?
            Light grows blunt in the sag of your flooded girth.
            Your claws are poison thorn.

Through slits of dragon-beak
he pants until the ragged clouds coagulate.
            Blades of grass grow sharp and splinter into frost.
            His stranded-jellyfish eye is open for business.

You shuffle and twitch as puddles leak their fill
and thickened rain goes muttering down the pipe.
            I think I hear you listen
            as I sift the grains of sleep.

Squinting sun can't scrape him out.
Fast as a stone of ice he will not budge.
            Each year I wait until I see his skin across the sky,
            and then I know: the moon toad has returned.

Potsherds

Digging in the garden I find them –
like words that have fallen out of use,
or someone's tooth wrapped in silver foil.

They make no sense but show either
a snapped pattern in blue or else
plain cream like a shattered cloud.

Laying them out on the workbench I see
their splintering tilt and shift into one
island of little fields. When I stick them

together my glue is a hawthorn hedge –
when I drink from stained-glass cups
of crazy-paving it tastes of rain.

Sunk constellations of crockery wait
for my trowel. A quiver of seagulls overhead
is something dashed to pieces but still flying.

On Being Invisible

Imagine an icicle underwater –
a chill of shimmer-bone in the stream, quickened

to the squirming glair of a glass eel:
that's how it is with me. Sleek in the can't-be-seen

but-always-here, I rest and let
the ripples of light pass through. Like a tumbler

of cold water poured into a lake,
I don't raise a murmur in the mirror. Gone so far

this time I can't come back, thin
as the window you gaze through to see if I'm here,

I've emptied myself away. Speak
to me sometimes if you like, by all means call my name –

I'll reply with crumbs on a plate
a mug in the sink and one wet footprint on the doorstep.

Instar

Follow the xylophone of the spine
down to where the bird-skull coccyx
calls my lost tail to come home,

and you'll find where it starts
like a snag in silk, a tear heading north
and widening – as I cross my arms

and reach behind my head, to shrug
a slim sack that tugs against me.
I've given up trying to keep them,

counting the erratic beats of a wilful heart –
instead I step from my legs and kick
off my toes, leaving myself behind

in order to find me, as it peels in warm
wrinkles I will throw away. Tonight
I'll be eased towards whatever comes next,

but now from winged shoulders I moult
my arms like two sleeves, shuck this sagging
suit of spilt skin, and plucking it past my ears

where it tends to catch, slough my face
until I am made over – then one by slow one
pull new fingers out of their hands.

Water Avens

I carry their scent from the steering wheel up the stairs –
    by morning the cuts on my fingers have all healed.

Foxglove

In large doses, the action of Digitalis on the circulation will cause various cerebral symptoms, such as seeing all objects blue.

Barbut's cuckoo-bee is lapis lazuli
      & the daisy carpenter-bee has cobalt wings.

The Ilfracombe humble-bee is Alice or beryl
      & the sparrow's eye is a pool of lavender rain.

You've licked the ultramarine of sour ink
      & dropped a fleck of smalt to stain your sight.

So your hands are cerulean now with turquoise nails
      & your face is a portrait drawn with midnight crayon.

The thought of what you've done is robin's egg
      & your veins are tangled roots which smell of Curaçao.

Tonight you'll lie in a bed of Turnbull's Blue
      & a swarm of gentian bees will sting you to sleep.

The Garden's Conversation with Darkness

Nine

You begin with the deft steps of a dusk-footed cat
      who dabs the fence with a pad
         of silent ink-drops.

Over the page it's taken all day to erase
      he prints the neat spoors of his black name –
         shadow-smoke, smutch-soot, dayligone.

His charcoal purr's the undertow
      of voices on a pillow. He leaves me awash
         in a murmur of ash.

Eleven

When daises clasp over in a green fist
      and every vanilla petal
         is smoothed into place

(until the flower-node is gripped fast)
      I dream sometimes that each pale spur
         turns into a frond alive with uplift

and each shut daisy becomes a moth
      who blossoms into flight and shivers
         on a waft of scent.

One

Moon is a glinting longbow
      taut with cold. It flowers into ear
          and swollen is the wizened skull

of a drowned god: his battered face
      a glimmer of melted lemon;
          his voice a dusty whisper.

Brittle as bleached shell,
      he won't go back to sleep until
          I give him a sip of water.

Three

You deep me with frost as autumn floats
      for a moment then goes under.
          Blackberries soak you up

and shoals of leaves must learn to swim
      the flood of your pull before
          being stranded by morning.

Rusty with ice they list like sodden boats
      on barnacled hulls, a final cargo of hailstones
          melting in the hold.

Five

You spoil me with mulberry, damson, plum –
        lull me in a crow's wing-beat,
                shut my bright in the deep

tar sleep of a bottomless well.
        You pick apart the stitch
                of apricot and peach.

I hold you close in the helpless mess
        I'm held in although I know
                you'll be gone tomorrow.

Seven

Landfall's a breath I take
        by coming awake. Your upsurge
                seeps and there beneath an ease

I find my arrival. Along the stippled strand
        a buttercup's open shell
                is a glance to waver gold

against my skin. Beachcombing blackbirds
        stab at the grist of a star –
                sparrows alight on my foreshore.

Petrichor

After a long spell of dry weather
it arrives with the first shower: I swallow

cool air in deep lungfuls of soft light –
and let the smell of petrichor release

a kind of inner rain, which leaves me full
to the brim with summer warmth that's been

and gone – and breathes me fresh, as if
preparing the ground for what's to come.

CHARLES BENNETT is widely acclaimed. **Evenlode**, his ninth collection, cemented his reputation as a lyrical landscape poet of depth and passion. Together with his intriguing new pamphlet **Thaw** and the ground-breaking 2019 collection **Cloud River**, he demonstrates gifts of vivid imagery and a deeply musical imagination. His work with choral composer Bob Chilcott has seen him hailed as a memorable and mesmerising librettist. He is writer-in-residence at Wicken Fen and combines this with his duties at the University of Northampton where he leads the BA in Creative Writing. He lives on the edge of Northamptonshire and Leicestershire with his wife, daughter and Labrador.

Brimming over with startling voices, arresting images and an indefatigable joie de vivre.
Poetry Book Society

Previous publications by Charles Bennett:

The Storm Bell, 1998
William Wordsworth's Socks, 2000
The Mermaid Room, 2000
Wintergreen, 2002
How to Make a Woman Out of Water, 2007
365 Apples, 2009
Orchard Days, 2009
Angry Planet, 2012
Evenlode, 2013

Forthcoming…

Cloud River 2019